Not Invisible:

Living & Learning Poetry Collection 2022

Dedicated to the children of Ukraine,

most especially,

those with disabilities.

My name is Katherine Stenzel. I graduated from Schoolcraft College with my Associates Degree in Fine Arts in May 2021. I have been writing poems for at least 4 years. My favorite hobbies are bike riding, taking nature walks with my mother, adult coloring books, and watching documentaries on Netflix and Amazon Prime. I love reading any book I can get my hands on - history, fiction, fairy tale collections, and various mythology books. I consider myself spiritual at heart, since I love exploring different avenues - which includes reading about magic, horoscopes, and mysticism.

Invisible

Somewhere in the shade,
I know you are there.
You claim to be invisible,
That you deserve to hide yourself away,
But I say, "That's not meant to be!"
I know a soul
That deserves to shine brightly.
I know a voice
That is meant to be heard.
I know a heart
That is very good,
That people must know is good.
Don't hide because you can't fit in.
Show yourself because
You can make a difference

Hell crammed full, Heaven deserted

The gates are open
Yet the space is empty.
Hell is crammed with sinners
And those who are sick in body
(Yet not sick in their souls)
Are too diseased to enter Heaven
And their list of sins
Too little to be condemned to the bottom.
There is nowhere for them to go.

Freeing of Soul from Body

I feel myself grow light...
My human body falls to the sand
As I take flight into the next journey.
These organs that made up
My mortal form –
My brain, my heart,
My joints, my limbs –
They all caused me
A lifetime of agony.
My spirit, too, was afflicted,
But now – I feel myself free!
Free for the next journey,
Free, perhaps, for eternal rest.

Looking for Angels, Running from Ghosts

All of us want to show our angels
But we all have our own ghosts.
But what about the angels and ghosts
That come from without?
For Angels, there is Heaven
But graveyards are the ghosts' domain.
When Angels appear
Heaven uses time and dreams
To give humans messages
Although the true purpose
Does not make itself clear.
In response, humans misunderstand the meaning
And struggle to understand
Whether it's for themselves or other people.
As for Ghosts,
They have messages from the grave;
Like the Angels, the position is a mystery.
Are Ghosts here to warn us
Against our oncoming doom,
Or are they here to haunt us forever,
Reminding us of our sins?
We are constantly questioning
If Angels and Ghosts exist
And why they are on earth
And what their positions and roles are…

Desert of Ice and Snow

Glittering snow
Ice as clear as glass…
From the rocky shores
To the frozen Lake St. Clair,
The frozen desert
Is a winter universe.
Frozen ice on the waves
Large ice as broken glass,
As if a chandelier
Had shattered to the floor.
Spanning mile upon mile
Is a desert of frozen water,
Of frozen lake water,
Of snow as shifty as sand in the wind,
Of ice as hard as chandelier glass
A wasteland of cold,
But a splendid view of beauty.

The Dark Chaos Down Below

I am close to water's edge
On the verge of discovering
The tumultuous core of the earth's conscious mind.
The waves look hungry now,
The highest of them bigger enough
To form a monstrous mouth
To swallow me whole.
It is terrifying in its vastness,
But boldly, I dive down deep.
The depths are much darker
Than it shows on the surface.
The cause of an innermost storm
Is the raging chaos below.
The surface is only
An outward reflection
Of the chaos dwelling down below.
It is dangerous to dive down deep,
But those that do –
Are they inwardly brave
Or completely foolish?

Turquoise Waters

Turquoise waters
You invite all that come over
Into your wet covers,
Using your blue-green color
And your gentle lapping sounds,
Which, combined with the cooling breeze,
Soothes the ears
As well as the fevered mind.
My joy.

Universe Bracelet

When I wear this bracelet,
I feel the universe
Comforting me.
The tiny stones around my wrist
Are like a galaxy of stars
Formed in living color.
I feel the stones
Whispering magic into my hand,
Through my wrist
And up into my arm.
There is a sense of peace –
And hidden power –
Within these tiny beads
And with them, I feel protected.

<u>**Snowing on All Hallows Day**</u>

All Hallows Day starts
With a little bit of snow
Sprinkling from the sky;
A rather surprising occurrence
When coming out of Halloween.
I wonder if the snow
Is some sort of message…

Phoenix

With the sun rising
On a new chapter of life,
Whatever passes
Is reborn in its place.
Maintaining balance
Within the life cycle.
One star is born in the sky
And another is born on this earth.
You are that star,
The phoenix who arises
From the ashes of the end.
Wherever I am,
Wherever I go,
I hear your calling,
But they are coming
From all sides of this globe.
This is your way
Of letting me know
That no matter where I go,
Your calling –
Your voice,
Your spirit –
Is constantly by my side.
No, it is within me –
My heart,
My soul,
My joy.

My name is Jared Brda, and this is the second time I have contributed to a Living & Learning collection. Individually, I have worked on a collection with a poem for each day of the year, and for this book I decided to select my personal favorite from each month, making twelve poems in total, which is one more than my last contribution. You can watch videos where I read them on my YouTube channel Jared Jams to see if you agree with me. I hope you will enjoy reading these poems as much as I enjoyed writing them, and maybe I can teach you a thing or two about some of my favorite subjects.

I send you hope, take it everywhere.

Poem chosen for January 1st:
<u>A New Beginning</u>

In the beginning, there was the word.
I am winning, haven't you heard?
A new time has begun,
The old one is done,
And now let's have fun!

We have a limited time,
So why not enjoy it while it lasts?
Do what you will,
Showcase your skill,
Live for the thrill!

But you can also be chill,
If that is what you will.
It doesn't all have to be excitement,
And only just frightment,
Sometimes it is best to take it slow.

Other times you may want to go,
And if the mood is right, I say,
Make it so!

And while things don't always turn out how we plan,
I say, in your life, try to have as much fun as you can,
Because you never know, when it's going to end!

Poem chosen for February 5th:
Valiance

Hey, why not go
All the way back,
Perhaps, 1993?
Please, bear with me, it's not the last that
Year will be seen.

Before I continue,
I will explain, that there's
Room for more than one
Thing to make this day special, I
Hope that is plain.
During this time, I got an idea for a book.
And I hope you will take a look.
Yet, that book is not the only thing

Very important to me.
Awhile back, a
Life was begun. I hope it will be
Eventful and fun.
Really hope she appreciates my wish,
I made these words to max and mish,
Ensuring that both these things are honored, as this
poem has its finish!

Poem chosen for March 5th:
<u>The Most Special Day</u>

If this poem seems especially long, that is because I intentionally made it 1,999 words to match up with my birth year, to fit with the poem for my birthday. Don't worry, all the ones after this are *much* shorter!

I hope to achieve all of my goals,
And among them includes growing old.
I have many stories to be told, and I want to live long enough to see them all unfold.

There is a special day that we put aside,
But from this day I used to hide.
I hope you will allow me to confide, to you, the feelings that grew.

I used to resent getting older,
Though in recent years I have grown a little bolder.
But I used to have a chip on my shoulder.
But to these thoughts I will give an unfolder.

When I was a little pup, my greatest fear
Was growing up. Truth be told, I was scared of the adult world,
To me it seemed very distant and cold, and I dreaded growing another year old.

I understand that achievements were unlocked,
But you may be shocked, to find, that this
Was actually a negative in my mind.
Not to be unkind, but if we rewind, I hope you will find,
My reasoning.

I felt I was ready, and that I was steady,
For the things that I was not allowed.
But since I felt others were petty, and I still used a
teddy, I did not say them aloud.
The fact that I kept these to myself, of that I am not
proud, and now I don't know if I found the right crowd.
These thoughts were left in a shroud, but now I will
tell you what I was talking about.

I did not want to wait to be on my own,
Though I did hate the world of the grown.
I did not mind when their stuff was shown,
But I thought I was ready to leave my home.
I did not want to wait eight more years,
And this was a time before my fears,
Took over, and of what was good for me, I thought I
was a knower.

Despite my meekness, I thought I had uniqueness,
I thought I needed no repentance, for my desire of
independence,
I felt like some would make an accusation, because of
my motivation.
In all fairness, I thought I had more awareness.
I did not find it a rarity, for those of my kind to find
prosperity.
I felt that my creations, manifestations, would be
enough, and that I could easily get through the parts
that were rough.
I sure did think that I was tough!

But I did not go beyond what was inside of my head.
I just sat around and continued to dream instead.
And lived this fantasy life safe from my bed.
And reality I still would dread.

But I guess, that it was for the best,
I did not try to test my luck.
And I am glad, that the state that was bad, I am no longer stuck,
And they are no longer here to run amuck.

But now this day is a highlight for me.
I get many gifts for free,
And unlike the day with the gifts under the tree,
ALL of the gifts go to me!
But the older I get, the harder it is to forget,
That I could have gotten those gifts all on my own,
Now that I am among the grown.

But never mind that,
Unlike a cat, my lives do not go up to nine,
There is only one of mine, and I try to be fine,
With all of that.

I view it like leveling up,
And I will probably be a grup,
as my age goes up and up,
But this will be made easier if I watch what I sup.

I will hopefully gain more knowing,
As I am growing,
And I keep throwing,
These parties for the day of my birth,
And I will be showing, what I am worth,
And I can measure my life's girth,
And how I have spent my time here on Earth.
Hopefully my accomplishments will be unearthed,
By the time I am done,
And I have increased the level of fun,
For the citizens of this planet,
At least that is the way that I plan it.

There are times where I may want to can it,
But those times don't last forever,
But life, I never want to damn it, with faint praise,
I don't want to remember all of my days,
As just a time I was left in a haze,
I want happiness to be a craze!

But this is one of those days,
Where my mind plays,
With those thoughts,
And the things that have broughts, these sorts of
thoughts to me.
Evidently I am a fan of fun, especially on the Day of
the Sun,
And on it I want to go and run, and forget any wrong
that was done.

Maybe I seem a bit centered on the self,
But I think we all deserve a day to ourself.
Though I may not live as long as that Grand-Elf,
I will spend as much time as I have improving myself.

The biggest issue of all you see,
Is the expectation, to me.
One of the only things worse than a bad day,
Is one that you hoped to be good and did not turn out
how it should.
I pray that nothing bad happens on my day,
But if it does, then I will have to find another way, to
honor the day.

Say, I do like to play, though some may say I am too
old to enjoy myself that way.
To them I say: "Hey! It is not your business the way
that I spend my day.

Now all I have left to say, is to go your own way, and only come back another day,
When you appreciate the value of play, and will no longer say, things to darken up my day!"

But assuming that it all goes well, hopefully there will be good things to tell.
A great cake we can make, good presents to be present, and be presented,
And a person to be represented, on their special day.
Good things to be given, to the person still livin',
Who is chillin', and improving their skillin'.
Please, don't act like a villain,
Just for some thrillin'.
Don't let me slip, on my ego trip,
Please get a grip, on how much this means to me!

I dreamt of the past,
But that dream did not last.
To the future I look ahead,
Although in that future I will be dead.
But I have heard it say,
That a gift is today,
And that is why the present, it is described in that way.
That you will view time in this way, I do pray, because it is a much calmer way,
To look at the day.

But one advice I have for you is to not resist, the possibility that,
You may not get everything that is on your list.
Do not put your hand in a fist, if every single thing does not go your way,
On your special day. I hope that you may, take this advice to heart.

And this will be a good start, to go about your way.

Before you go about eating your special dish,
You are expected to make your birthday wish.
You may wish for that special dish, or some other
thing for fortune to bring.
They say not to tell anyone, and I guess that is part of
the fun,
And you can wish for anything under the sun!

I have told you that now is not forever,
And I think it is for the better,
If you remember this sentiment.
It is for the betterment,
Of your life.
Just because you may not want to get older,
Does not mean that you have to stay colder, to the
day that celebrates this fact,
But at the end of the day, I say, it is up to you, how
you want to act.
It is your choice of how to react, to the attention you
bring,
And to the people who sing, for you to be happy on
the day of your birth,
And celebrate your life on top of this Earth.

A part of me views it as an accomplishment, that I had
made it this far.
Though it is a bit melancholy, and something of a
folly, to be happy about the others that did not.
But I do not choose to accept that thought, only to be
happy that I have been brought, this far,
And I can be made to feel like a star. I feel that deep
down, most of us are, though it may not have been
brought out all of the time,
Thus far.

But after all, it is just another day of the year, and it is
up to you how much you want to cheer.

Although they say that age is just a number, but I can
not slumber, on the fact that is not entirely true.
Are there differences between ages 5 and 55 to you?
Or 2 and 22? Did your perceptions skew?
It may not be exactly as important as we make it out
to be, but please listen to me, it does mean something
to an extent.
It is something of a significant event.

I realize some day that I will be joining with the
angels,
And that my perceptions will be newfangled.
These thoughts, they have been dangled, in front of
me,
But I hope that that day will not come for me, for a
long while,
And in the meantime I will try to cause a smile.

I am devoted to this cause,
Though sometimes I have to stop and pause,
And observe the flaws, I see all around me.
But I am not bound to these,
Though time, it does freeze,
And sometimes it is a breeze,
But when I observe the trees,
I realize how shortly I have been around compared to
them.
And sometimes my thoughts have been repaired to
hem.
I know that my place in this world is limited, and
hopefully in that time I'll be givin' it, my all,
Before the day I fall,

I hope I have given harm to none and blessings to all.

I know that I may not do every single thing that I set
out to do,
But hopefully I can give an example out to you,
Of the things that you at least *can* do, throughout your
life,
Not everything, but just enough to suffice.
I hope that alone is nice, and that being nice is
enough to suffice,
And you do not think it vice, and it will not be a big
price, for you to pay,
To act in the kindly way.

I hope you are willing to still believe, in the good
things you can receive,
If you begin to adopt this way, to look at the day.
It is no guarantee that things will always be good,
But I think that you should, at least see a little bit of
improvement,
And you don't need me to prove it, I think deep down
inside we all knew it.
Though some went and blew it. They twisted and
began to screw it.
But hopefully you will show them the right way to
behave. I hope you will do it!

As you can see, this day causes a lot of feelings in
me,
But hopefully writing all this will have set me free,
From the thoughts that have been troubling me.

But I guess all things have their good and their bad,
Pretty much anything can make you both happy and
sad,
I guess anything can be both sappy and rad.

Things can be joyful and make you glad, or be crappy
and make you mad,

True, this composition.
Mopefully I put myself in this position, but
Hopefully my states are no longer in competition, and
Hopefully the cycle has come to completion.

Poem chosen for April 1st:
<u>Your April Fool</u>

I really thought,
You would be gone,
From my head by now.
But in my dreams, you always seem,
To come back somehow.

When I think of how you perceived me,
I could assume, but,
You know exactly,
What that makes out of you and me.

The feeling I got when I awoke,
Was like the world was pulling some kind of joke.

My fear for you is my anxiety's tool,
And it's like I'm your April Fool.

Even though we haven't seen each other in years,
I still remember my tears.

Of my pain, you were not the cause.
But, I refused to accept your flaws.

It's not your fault that you are seeped into my brain,
And that it likes to remind me of my pain.

They say that there are plenty of fish in the sea,
But that everyone is unique, and that doesn't make
sense to me.

There is only one you, what I could not do, is find
another.

But I am hoping that someone who had what I liked in you, can be my lover.

This is the plague of OCD, this is not the last time I'll write about thee,
I just hope that my mind's version of you will leave me be,
And no more charms will fool me!

Poem chosen for May 26th:
<u>Be the Person You are Looking For</u>

I know that most of us want perfection for us to see,
but what if I told you, that it is better for perfect to *be*?
We want someone, who is in good spirit and good
health,
But I want you to hear it: that the someone you should
be trying to improve, is *yourself*.
You may be thinking that there is nothing wrong, and
if that's *truly* the case, then you had it within you all
along!

For we all have true potential, and self discovery is
essential, for trying to improve the outer world.

I am just glad that this message has been told.

Poem chosen for June 11th:
<u>Ariana</u>

About 1993,
Really pretty sight to see.
I was not yet born, but when I first saw your face I
Adored you.
Nevermind the groundbreaking adventure,
All I cared about was you, the girl who gave me
Tremors.

Come a few years later, it was time to cheer.
Leading your way into our hearts,
And later you made works of arts.
Riding along, and ever since,
I wanted to be your Stallion Prince.
Care not I for Murphy's Law,
Even if scratched by a

Raptor's claw,
It would be worth it to be with you.
Cheerfully my heart begins to cry. My
Heart is singing, and
Ariana, You're the
Reason why.
Devoted, these words have been to you, and I'd be
lucky to find
Someone even half as good as you!

Poem chosen for July 26th:
<u>The Lady from Across the Pond</u>

Let it be known that I am very fond
Of this lady from across the pond.
Noble and Kind, and in a world of my own,
This lady would be mine.

I would be her beau,
And her Very Good Advice I would follow.
I hope her Mother and Mine would allow,
And the Leader we would also Follow.

In our Lands we will Never Wonder,
For in there we will always under-
Stand one another.

We could Waltz the night away,
I could save her from the pirates led astray.
Never entering the world of the grown,
We'd have fun forever in this world of our own,
If everything Pans out the way that I want it to,
As I spend time On an Island with You!

It could get quite Windy,
But if she would befriend me,
Then I would not care.

If this important date comes soon,
Say,
Four O'clock in the afternoon,
Could we share a toon?

And we could rule our noble subjects there!
Happy Un-Birthday to my Queen,
And how I love to hear my fair lady sing!

This Lost Boy is happy that he found you,
And maybe he can help you find your White Rabbit
too.
We could Jabber and Walk,
I could grab her and talk,
And travel we must,
For all we need is: Faith, Trust, and a little Pixie
Dust!*

Those with character like you,
They seem to be very few.

And while these feelings are true,
The real world doesn't give me as much to do.

I could still pretend, but at points,
This fantasy has to end.
We are years and lands apart,
And it wouldn't be good for me to start,
Believing in the things I imagined.

By this I am saddened,
But I hope someday we can be companioned,
In a Wonderful Never Land of our own!

*Quote from *Peter Pan* by J.M. Barrie

Poem chosen for August 20th:
<u>My Father's Day</u>

1. I never knew you,
2. And writing this may be bold,
3. For you left this world when I was two months old.
4. I'm sure I was precious to you, and that you cared.
5. That must be why your middle name was shared.
6. We love many of the same things,
7. From the Stars, Dragons, Beats, and Rings.
8. The Beast didn't give you,
9. A chance to raise me.
10. The game of thrones was played,
11. With those who prayed,
12. To his enemy, and faced the sword.
13. I don't remember if I shed any tears,
14. But I hope you can be with him a thousand years,
15. Jesus, our Lord!

Poem chosen for September 28th:
<u>Melancholy Desert</u>
(A tribute to the victims of The Holodomor)

1 I cannot say the names of the nameless.

1 Millions of people,
2 Exterminated by hunger, and
3 They were all swept under,
4 The rug, and mass graves dug,
5 Except in the places in which they were not
allowed.
6 They were executed if found keeping grain,
7 And terror, it was to reign.
8 To survive, they would have to steal.
9 But if caught, they would die, on the order of the
man of steel.

1 The father of the peoples believed they had sinned,
2 He chased them with a sword, and anger spent.
3 After inflicting punishment, he let the survivors
scatter in the winds.

1 His will could only be satisfied,
2 If his fury would finally subside,

1 But history seems to show that it lasted until the day
he died.

1 For two years there was famine in the land,
2 And the fathers and mothers had to say goodbye to
the children they had cared for,
3 For what had happened by His hand.
4 Because they were subjected to this horrid time,
5 They had to witness such horrid crimes.
6 Because this nation held so much grain,

7 Stalin would starve all of Ukraine.
8 The homeland laid to waste,
9 The death machine upped with haste.

1 The policies Ioseb enacted were sadistic,
2 But the apathy may have proved him right,
3 "One death a tragedy, one million a statistic"*

1 For those who suffered, the world would never be
the same, but I just hope
2 That I have brought awareness to their pain,
3 So that the millions who died shall not have died in
vain!

*Paraphrased quote attributed to Joseph Stalin,
though its origin hasn't been confirmed.

Poem chosen for October 1st:
<u>That Time of the Year</u>

It is that time of the year,
The time of fear,
And the time of cheer.

Costumes ranging from horrible,
Spooky, funny, to adorable.
The time where we prepare, regardless of how wise
To cause a scare and put on a disguise.

There is a feeling of "umph,"
All throughout this month.
And I consider it a triumph,
If it all goes well.

I admit, my expectations have gotten high,
And that is the reason why,
This season that I love so,
Also gives me feelings of anxious woe.

For while it reminds me of when I could unhinge,
It also brings up memories that make me cringe.
I like to party on that special day,
And it does feel hearty in that special way.
I want these parties to be as good as can be,
But trying too hard puts a lot of pressure on me.

Hopefully I will get these feelings fixed,
But for now, I'll describe them as "mixed."
I guess it depends on what mood I am in,
And some may consider it a sin,
But I say, as long as no harm is done,
I wish a Happy Halloween Season to everyone,
Besides those who prefer not to celebrate,

October 30 + 1
Poem chosen for November 30th:
<u>The Mysterious Stranger (inspired by the Mark Twain</u>
<u>story of the same name)</u>

The forest is where our journey began.
Out there in the wild, we found that perfect child.
I don't know why us he picked, but he charmed us
with his magic tricks.
For we were nothing but ants accord-
Ing to that Angel of the Lord.

He created people, for us to play.
He created humans, he made them out of clay.
He destroyed the people, he took them all away.
He could create more people, on another day.

He altered what would happen at the stream,
But it did not matter, for life is but a dream.
We will never forget the day we met our young friend
Phillip Traum, and how he made our friend drown.
That saved him from a lifelong scar, for you see,
He was interested, not in good and evil, or how things
should be, but in things *as they are.*

This may seem intense, but that is only because you
have the moral sense.
This may have trouble entering your brain,
But in some cases death is a merciful thing.

Time he turned, and accused witches we saw burned.
"It is inhumane" says you, but cruelty is the human
thing to do.
You may wonder, "where is the moral sense of his?"
But he can do no wrong, for he does not know what it
is.

We revel, in the words of that nephew of The Devil.

I hoped that I would escape strife when I entered the
next life, but then he'd soon reveal, that that life
wasn't real.

Nothing would I feel, for nothing is truly real.

But you won't have to worry about being someone
that time forgot,
For nothing truly exists but you.
And you, are but a thought.*

*Quote from *The Mysterious Stranger* by Mark Twain.

Poem chosen for December 31st:
<u>An Old End</u>

Those were my poems,
I hope they gave you cheer.
I made one for each day of the year.
Some were made to get through a fear,
Some to help shed a tear,
But all were for people to hear.

I hope I gave you all a good time,
As all of these poems were uniquely mine.
I tried to speak of all the things that I am interested in,
Ever since I decided to begin,
This project.
But if you did not, and happiness was not brought,
To you, through it,
Do not feel ashamed if I knew it.
We don't all have to like the same things, but I hope
an interesting experience was gained,
Through taking part in it.
If you think you can make something better, I
encourage it,
This project has given me courage. It,
Made me feel better about expressing myself,
Before it, I used to be secretive, and worried that I'd
be judged,
If I said the things that I truly feel.
But now, I feel more comfortable, being able to reveal,
Through my creative works, the things that I have
decided to seal,
Up, and not share with anyone.
But now that the project is done,
I will end with a prayer to Holy Spirit, Father, and Son:

I thank you for this gift you have given me,

For the person you have made me be,
And for the works that my appreciators see.

I hope I have done you proud,
That these thoughts have been allowed,
And I have helped those who need it reach the ninth
cloud.

Kindness, I hope it was brought,
And the messages not forgot,
And that they all have joined me in thought.

Comfort, I know it was sought,
And through my writings I hope it was brought,
And of positive emotions, there was a lot.

Some of it may have been cheerful,
Some of it may have been fearful,
And some of us may have been tearful.

I know that you are good,
And I believe that I should,
Sing your praises.

I don't know if I could,
I just know that if I would,
I would use the most respectable of phrases.

I have given glimpses of my life,
The happy moments as well as the strife,
And shown them all of my phases.

They may now shed a tear,
Because it is the end of the year,
But please advise them to have no fear.

We will be back again, as my creative output is
becoming a trend.
But I won't deny him above the sky, forever then, I'll
say,

Amen.

My name is Malcolm Wang and I am a writer and creator. I am 21 years old. I am a resident of Northville. I love to sing, dance, read, write everyday, and go hiking in the woods. I am also an artist. I specialize in nature photography.

Poems:

Titanium

1. Titanium blue
2. My favorite mineral
3. Canada crystal

Elevator

1. I scrape the sky high
2. On level seventy two
3. Renaissance Center

Topaz

1. Topaz is a song
2. I see it in museums
3. Orange crystal blue

Sunset

1. At sunset, on bikes
2. Swing, spin, climb, slide, together.
3. Thornton Creek playground

Power Outage

1. The power went out
2. When rain turns to ice, no heat
3. Snuggle to stay warm

I Believe

I believe in beauty
        in science
        in nature
I believe in love
        in kindness
        in mercy
I believe in words
        in truth
        in memory
I believe in riding elevators at malls
I believe in laughing on roller coasters
I believe in taking off my shirt and running in the
fountains
I believe in jumping in puddles in the rain
I believe in looking straight down from the top of a
skyscraper
I dream of Paris,
        going to the top of the Eiffel Tower
I dream of the Gateway arch in St. Louis, Missouri,
        the gateway is of my mind
I dream of the Burj Khalifa
        walking in the clouds
I am inspired by you

Lake Geneva

1. Hotel on the lake
2. On the boat, we had ice cream
3. Visit Grandpa's house

Roller Coasters

1. Gemini - 2 tracks
2. Race each other up and down
3. I feel energy

Thunder

1. Thunder woke me up
2. Pouring rain at six o'clock
3. But I stayed in bed

Parking Garage

1. Boats on the river
2. Beaubien parking garage
3. Up on level 4

Long Sleeves

1. Long sleeves feel safe, warm
2. Autumn, summer, spring, winter
3. Air on skin, too cold.

The Year with No Halloween

The Year with No Halloween
Was stolen by a grinch
People were upset about it
Everyone was crying
And were confused about it
Because they were not expecting it to happen

The Bird Who Migrated For The Winter

There once was a bird
Whose name was Sammy
And she went
To the rainforest
Where it was warm
To migrate
Just for the winter

Wait What

Wait What
What language is that lifeguard speaking in?
Its not English.
It was not French
And it was not Spanish.
So what language was it then?
I have no idea what language that lifeguard was
speaking in.
We were at the top of the waterslide
Just about to go down
And I noticed that
The lifeguard was
Speaking in a foreign language
He was not making any sense

I Want

I have always wanted to
>go to the Seattle Space Needle
>go to the Eiffel Tower in Paris, France
>go to the Washington Monument
>go to Traverse City
>go to Grand Canyon National Park
>go to Yellowstone National Park
>visit all the National Parks
>go to Holiday World
>go to Paris

I want
>friendship
>love
>comfort
>happiness
>positive thinking
>to go hiking

I want to
>be a writer
>be a gentleman
>have a good heart
>go hiking
>hike the Marsh Trail
>hike #1-5 at Legacy Park

In Paris,
>I want to go to the top when I go to the top
>when I go to the Eiffel Tower someday
>because my grandparents went there and went
>to the second floor only and check out the
>Louvre Art Museum with the Mona Lisa.

At Grand Canyon National Park,

I want to hike to the bottom of the canyon
because that's what my grandparents did.
At Yellowstone National Park,
I want to check out the Grand Canyon of the
Yellowstone at Yellowstone National Park
because that's what my grandparents did.
I want to visit all the national parks someday
I want to check out Voyage coaster at Holiday World
because I really want to go there

Someday, I want to go to Dusseldorf,
get a boarding pass to get to the Dusseldorf
airport
check out the Dusseldorf Hauptbahnhof
go around the city in buses
walk along the bank of the Rhine River where
we can watch the ships, see many
castles, and mountains
visit the museum Kunstapalast on a Saturday
to check out Andy Warhol's photo "Joseph
Beyus"
take the bus to visit the castle tower,
Schlossturm
at Schlossturm, I want to climb up the steps
and go to the top to see the shipping museum
go to Bazzar Cafe for lunch
after dinner, dance with all my friends in an
area where there's so much space
stay at the Melia hotel that's 9 floors and check
into hotel and room is on the ninth floor, top
floor
Someday, I want to go to Italy
check out the Trevi Fountain
go to mass at St. Peter

        at St, Peter I want to climb up all the steps to
the top of the dome
I am full of ideas
I have thoughts, ideas and feelings just like you.

Thank you for supporting Living & Learning
Enrichment Center of Northville

The proceeds of this collection will go towards
the center and its beautiful cause